MW01242182

The Ultimate
Relationship Challenge

Over 300 'Would You Rather' Questions for Improving Relationships, Spicing Up Your Sex Life, and Creative Date Night Fun

Brittany Coy

Copyright © 2023 by Brittany Coy

Contents

Introduction   I

Trust & Commitment   2

Conflict   10

Sex & Intimacy   18

Work & Money   32

Family   41

Fun & Adventure   50

Growth & Spirituality   66

Dreams & Goals   74

Let's Recap   87

Introduction

Relationships are a delicate dance between two people, constantly evolving as they navigate through life together. Each relationship is unique, with its own set of joys, challenges, and experiences. However, there are certain universal themes that every couple must confront to build a strong and lasting bond. Trust, communication, conflict resolution, intimacy, and shared goals are just a few of these essential ingredients.

In this book, you will find a collection of thought-provoking "would you rather" questions designed to spark conversation, deepen your connection, and promote understanding and growth in your relationship. Each section of the book covers a different topic, including Trust & Commitment, Conflict, Sex & Intimacy, Work & Money, Family, Fun & Adventure, Growth & Spirituality, and Dreams & Goals.

Whether you are a new couple just starting your journey together or a long-term couple looking to rekindle the flame, these questions will encourage open and honest communication, promote intimacy, and help you better understand each other's wants, needs, and desires. So, if you are ready to take your relationship to the next level, grab a copy of this book, and let the conversation begin!

Trust & Commitment

Would you rather have complete transparency with your partner or keep some things private?

Would you rather be in a long-distance relationship for a year or be apart from your partner for six months every year?

Would you rather be with someone who has cheated in the past but has changed, or someone who has always been faithful but has other flaws?

Would you rather have your partner go through your phone or go through theirs?

Would you rather have a partner who is always honest but sometimes blunt, or one who is tactful but occasionally lies?

Would you rather have your partner know all of your passwords or keep them private?

Would you rather have a partner who is clingy or one who is distant?

Would you rather know all of your partner's exes or never hear about them?

Would you rather have your partner spend time with their ex or have them cut all ties?

Would you rather have a partner who values their independence or one who is always available to you?

Would you rather have your partner tell you about their past relationships or keep that information private?

Would you rather have your partner be completely open about their feelings or have them keep some things to themselves?

Would you rather have your partner admit to lying or hide the truth to protect your feelings?

Would you rather have a partner who is jealous or one who trusts you completely?

Would you rather have your partner choose you over their career or choose their career over you?

Would you rather have a partner who is a workaholic or one who prioritizes their relationship?

Would you rather have a partner who is spontaneous or one who plans everything out?

Would you rather have your partner be your best friend or someone you have a strong physical connection with?

Would you rather have your partner spend time with their friends or always be with you?

Would you rather have a partner who wants to get married soon or one who wants to wait?

Would you rather have a partner who wants children or one who doesn't?

Would you rather have a partner who is always on their phone or one who disconnects when spending time with you?

Would you rather have your partner share all your interests or have some differences to keep things interesting?

Would you rather have your partner move to be with you or move to be with them?

Would you rather have a partner who is very outgoing or one who is more introverted?

Would you rather have your partner surprise you with gifts or be more practical with their spending?

Would you rather have a partner who is always punctual or one who is more relaxed about time?

Would you rather have your partner plan all the dates or share the responsibility?

Would you rather have a partner who is very affectionate or one who is more reserved?

Would you rather have a partner who is very traditional or someone who is more progressive?

Would you rather have your partner be your mentor or your equal?

Would you rather have a partner who is very organized or one who is more relaxed?

Conflict

Would you rather have a partner who always agrees with you or one who challenges you?

Would you rather have a partner who avoids conflict or one who confronts it head-on?

Would you rather have a partner who always apologizes first or one who waits for you to apologize?

Would you rather have a partner who wants to talk about every issue or one who lets some things go?

Would you rather have a partner who takes criticism well or one who gets defensive?

Would you rather have your partner express their emotions through words or actions?

Would you rather have a partner who is quick to forgive or one who holds grudges?

Would you rather have your partner express their anger or keep it bottled up?

Would you rather have a partner who needs time alone to cool down or one who wants to talk things out right away?

Would you rather have your partner be very passionate during arguments or one who remains calm?

Would you rather have a partner who can admit when they're wrong or one who always thinks they're right?

Would you rather have your partner use humor to diffuse tense situations or be serious?

Would you rather have a partner who is very logical during arguments or one who is more emotional?

Would you rather have your partner compromise or stand their ground during disagreements?

Would you rather have a partner who is always willing to talk things out or one who needs time to process?

Would you rather have a partner who brings up past issues during arguments or one who focuses on the present?

Would you rather have a partner who seeks outside help during conflicts or one who wants to handle things on their own?

Would you rather have your partner be empathetic or unsympathetic during arguments?

Would you rather have a partner who is more passive or one who is more assertive during conflicts?

Would you rather have your partner compromise on some things or always give in?

Would you rather have your partner bring up sensitive topics during arguments or avoid them altogether?

Would you rather have your partner be honest even if it hurts or lie to spare your feelings?

Would you rather have a partner who is willing to apologize even if they don't think they're wrong or one who never apologizes?

Would you rather have your partner take responsibility for their actions or make excuses?

Would you rather have your partner express their feelings calmly or with anger?

Would you rather have a partner who is willing to listen to your side or one who is stubborn and refuses to budge?

Would you rather have your partner be willing to compromise or one who always wants to have things their way?

Would you rather have a partner who is willing to admit their faults or one who always thinks they're right?

Would you rather have your partner bring up issues right away or wait until they've built up?

Would you rather have your partner be solution-oriented or one who dwells on the problem?

Would you rather have a partner who can see your perspective or one who is always thinking about themselves?

Would you rather have your partner be willing to make changes or one who is set in their ways?

Sex & Intimacy

Would you rather have sex in the morning or at night?

Would you rather have a quickie or a long, slow session?

Would you rather have sex in a romantic setting or a more spontaneous one?

Would you rather have sex with lots of foreplay or skip right to the main event?

Would you rather have sex with lots of kissing or more physical touch?

Would you rather have sex with lots of dirty talk or more sensual talk?

Would you rather have sex with one partner or multiple partners?

Would you rather have sex with your partner's fantasy or your own?

Would you rather have sex in a monogamous or open relationship?

Would you rather have sex with more frequent or less frequent?

Would you rather have sex with lots of positions or a few go-to favorites?

Would you rather have sex with lots of eye contact or closed eyes?

Would you rather have sex with lots of intimacy or more casual sex?

Would you rather have sex with lots of touching or more penetration focused?

Would you rather have sex with lots of oral sex or less focus on it?

Would you rather have sex with lots of feedback or less communication?

Would you rather have sex with lots of focus on your own pleasure or your partner's?

Would you rather have sex with lots of emotional connection or more physical connection?

Would you rather have sex with someone who is vocal or quiet?

Would you rather have sex with someone who likes to cuddle or someone who wants space afterwards?

Would you rather have sex with someone who likes to experiment or stick to the basics?

Would you rather have sex with someone who likes to take control or let you take the lead?

Would you rather have sex with someone who is open about their desires or someone who is more reserved?

Would you rather have sex with someone who likes to watch porn or doesn't?

Would you rather have sex with someone who likes to use sexual fantasies or prefers reality?

Would you rather be the one who initiates sex or wait for your partner to make the first move?

Would you rather use sex toys or rely solely on your bodies for pleasure?

Would you rather have sex for a long time or quickies more frequently?

Would you rather have sex on a regular schedule or when the mood strikes?

Would you rather explore each other's bodies slowly and sensually or get right down to business?

Would you rather have sex with the TV on or off?

Would you rather have sex with the windows open or closed?

Would you rather have sex with music playing or in silence?

Would you rather be the dominant partner or the submissive partner in bed?

Would you rather have sex in the shower or in the bathtub?

Would you rather have sex in a car or in a hotel room?

Would you rather have sex outdoors or indoors?

Would you rather have sex on a beach or in a pool?

Would you rather use role-playing to spice things up or keep it straightforward?

Would you rather experiment with bondage or keep things vanilla?

Would you rather have sex with the same person for the rest of your life or different people throughout your life?

Would you rather be tied up or do the tying?

Would you rather have sex with the lights on or only by candlelight?

Would you rather watch porn together or keep it separate?

Would you rather have sex before or after a romantic dinner?

Would you rather have sex in lingerie or in your birthday suit?

Would you rather have sex in a hot tub or a sauna?

Would you rather try out tantric sex or keep things more traditional?

Would you rather have sex while standing up or lying down?

Would you rather have sex in a hotel room or on a private yacht?

Would you rather have sex on the floor or on a bed?

Would you rather have sex in a tent or a cabin?

Would you rather have sex in a hot air balloon or on a train?

Would you rather have sex while skinny dipping or while wearing clothes?

Work & Money

Would you rather have a job that pays well but you don't enjoy, or a job that you love but doesn't pay much?

Would you rather work for a big corporation or a small startup?

Would you rather have a 9-5 job or work from home?

Would you rather work for a boss who is strict but fair, or a boss who is easygoing but unorganized?

Would you rather work with a team or work independently?

Would you rather work in a creative field or a technical one?

Would you rather have a job that requires a lot of travel or one that allows you to stay close to home?

Would you rather have a job with a lot of flexibility or one with a set schedule?

Would you rather work in a fast-paced environment or a more relaxed one?

Would you rather have a job with great benefits or a higher salary?

Would you rather have a job with a lot of job security or one with more room for growth?

Would you rather have a job that requires a lot of physical labor or one that is more mentally challenging?

Would you rather have a job that allows you to work outdoors or one that is office-based?

Would you rather work in a job that is very specialized or one that requires you to wear multiple hats?

Would you rather work in a job that is very demanding or one that allows for a good work-life balance?

Would you rather work in a job that is stable but boring or one that is exciting but unstable?

Would you rather work in a job that requires a lot of overtime or one that doesn't?

Would you rather work in a job that is more analytical or one that is more creative?

Would you rather have a job that is very prestigious or one that is more laid-back?

Would you rather work in a job that is more socially focused or one that is more solitary?

Would you rather have a job that allows for more autonomy or one that is more structured?

Would you rather have a job that allows you to work on your own terms or one that requires you to follow a set schedule?

Would you rather have a job that is very high pressure or one that is more relaxed?

Would you rather have a job that is more sales-oriented or one that is more service-oriented?

Would you rather have a job that requires a lot of communication or one that is more task-oriented?

Would you rather work in a job that requires a lot of training or one that you can learn as you go?

Would you rather work in a job that is more physically demanding or one that is more mentally taxing?

Would you rather work in a job that is very competitive or one that is more cooperative?

Would you rather work in a job that requires a lot of multitasking or one that is more focused?

Would you rather work in a job that requires a lot of attention to detail or one that is more broad-strokes?

Would you rather work in a job that requires you to be constantly learning or one that is more repetitive?

Would you rather work in a job that requires a lot of problem-solving or one that is more routine?

Would you rather work in a job that requires a lot of customer service or one that is more behind-the-scenes?

Would you rather work in a job that requires a lot of leadership or one that is more supportive?

Family

Would you rather have a big family or a small one?

Would you rather have children or remain childless?

Would you rather have a close-knit family or one that is more independent?

Would you rather have a family that lives close by or one that is spread out?

Would you rather spend holidays with your own family or your partner's family?

Would you rather have your parents live with you or live separately?

Would you rather have a family that is very traditional or one that is more progressive?

Would you rather have a family that is very involved in each other's lives or one that is more hands-off?

Would you rather have a family that is very opinionated or one that is more easygoing?

Would you rather have a family that is very religious or one that is more secular?

Would you rather have a family that is very outdoorsy or one that is more indoors?

Would you rather have a family that is very artistic or one that is more scientific?

Would you rather have a family that is very adventurous or one that is more risk-averse?

Would you rather have a family that is very health-conscious or one that is more relaxed about health?

Would you rather have a family that is very academic or one that is more focused on practical skills?

Would you rather have a family that is very political or one that is more apolitical?

Would you rather have a family that is very materialistic or one that is more focused on experiences?

Would you rather have a family that is very introverted or one that is more extroverted?

Would you rather have a family that is very intellectual or one that is more emotional?

Would you rather have a family that is very involved in each other's personal lives or one that is more private?

Would you rather have a family that is very competitive or one that is more collaborative?

Would you rather have a family that is very athletic or one that is more focused on intellectual pursuits?

Would you rather have a family that is very structured or one that is more free-spirited?

Would you rather have a family that is very spontaneous or one that is more predictable?

Would you rather have a family that is very outspoken or one that is more reserved?

Would you rather have a family that is very musical or one that is more focused on other hobbies?

Would you rather have a family that is very literary or one that is more focused on other forms of entertainment?

Would you rather have a family that is very focused on the past or one that is more future-oriented?

Would you rather have a family that is very tech-savvy or one that is more traditional?

Would you rather have a family that is very pet-friendly or one that is more focused on other interests?

Would you rather have a family that is very focused on physical appearance or one that is more focused on inner beauty?

Would you rather have a family that is very environmentally conscious or one that is more focused on other issues?

Would you rather have a family that is very focused on education or one that is more relaxed about it?

Would you rather have a family that is very interested in travel or one that is more content staying close to home?

Fun & Adventure

Would you rather travel to a new country every year or explore different parts of your own country?

Would you rather go on a road trip or take a cruise?

Would you rather go bungee jumping or skydiving?

Would you rather go camping in the wilderness or stay in a luxurious hotel?

Would you rather try a new adventurous activity every month or stick to familiar activities?

Would you rather go on a hiking trip or a beach vacation?

Would you rather go on a hot air balloon ride or a helicopter ride?

Would you rather go on a safari or go scuba diving in a coral reef?

Would you rather go on a cross-country road trip or backpack through Europe?

Would you rather go ziplining or rock climbing?

Would you rather try a new extreme sport or stick to safe activities?

Would you rather visit a theme park or a water park?

Would you rather take a cooking class or a dance class together?

Would you rather go on a city tour or a countryside tour?

Would you rather take a photography class or a painting class?

Would you rather visit a famous museum or a famous landmark?

Would you rather go skiing or snowboarding?

Would you rather take a boat tour or a helicopter tour?

Would you rather go on a hot air balloon ride or ride in a vintage car?

Would you rather go on a guided tour or explore on your own?

Would you rather go to a music festival or a comedy festival?

Would you rather go on a romantic getaway or a group trip with friends?

Would you rather go on a kayaking trip or a canoeing trip?

Would you rather go on a guided hike or a self-guided hike?

Would you rather visit a national park or a historical site?

Would you rather go on a sightseeing tour or a food tour?

Would you rather go on a wine tasting tour or a beer tasting tour?

Would you rather go on a nature walk or a garden tour?

Would you rather go on a horseback ride or a bike ride?

Would you rather go on a river rafting trip or a paddleboarding trip?

Would you rather go on a yoga retreat or a meditation retreat?

Would you rather go on a whale watching tour or a dolphin watching tour?

Would you rather go on a wildlife safari or a bird watching trip?

Would you rather go on a road trip or a train trip?

Would you rather go on a fishing trip or a hunting trip?

Would you rather go on a hot springs tour or a waterfall tour?

Would you rather go on a bike tour or a walking tour?

Would you rather travel to a new country every year or return to your favorite destination multiple times?

Would you rather backpack through the mountains or relax on a beach vacation?

Would you rather go on a road trip or take a flight to your destination?

Would you rather stay in a luxury hotel or a cozy bed and breakfast?

Would you rather visit historical landmarks or experience local culture through food and festivals?

Would you rather travel during peak season or off-season to avoid the crowds?

Would you rather stay in a resort with all-inclusive amenities or book accommodations and activities separately?

Would you rather visit a place with lots of adventure activities or a place with lots of relaxation activities?

Would you rather travel solo or with a group of friends?

Would you rather stay in a fancy hotel with a view or a unique accommodation like a treehouse or igloo?

Would you rather visit a place with a lot of nightlife or a more laid-back atmosphere?

Would you rather travel to a place with a warm or cold climate?

Would you rather visit a city known for its museums or its outdoor activities?

Would you rather travel to a place where you don't speak the language or a place where you're familiar with the language?

Would you rather travel to a place with a lot of shopping or a place with a lot of nature?

Would you rather visit a place with a lot of wildlife or a place with marine life?

Would you rather visit a place with a lot of outdoor markets or indoor malls?

Would you rather travel to a place with a lot of street food or a place with a lot of fine dining?

Would you rather visit a place with a lot of water activities or a place with a lot of mountain activities?

Would you rather stay in a place with a lot of privacy or a place with a lot of social interaction?

Would you rather visit a place with a lot of ancient ruins or a place with a lot of natural wonders?

Would you rather travel to a place with a lot of amusement parks or a place with a lot of cultural experiences?

Would you rather stay in a place with a lot of luxury amenities or a place with a more rustic charm?

Would you rather travel to a place with a lot of spiritual significance or a place with a lot of scientific importance?

Would you rather visit a place with a lot of art galleries or a place with a lot of live music venues?

Growth & Spirituality

Would you rather meditate together every day or read spiritual texts together?

Would you rather volunteer at a local charity or attend a religious service together?

Would you rather go on a pilgrimage or a meditation retreat?

Would you rather read spiritual books together or attend a spiritual study group?

Would you rather read a book on personal growth or attend a seminar on the topic?

Would you rather join a spiritual community or practice your faith privately?

Would you rather take a class on mindfulness or a class on manifestation?

Would you rather volunteer for a charity organization or donate money to a cause?

Would you rather journal your thoughts or have deep conversations about life with your partner?

Would you rather practice gratitude daily or practice forgiveness regularly?

Would you rather explore different belief systems or stick to your own beliefs?

Would you rather practice self-care or self-compassion?

Would you rather practice yoga together or take a dance class together?

Would you rather attend a personal development workshop or a self-help seminar?

Would you rather join a book club or attend a group meditation session?

Would you rather practice self-reflection or engage in deep conversations with your partner?

Would you rather explore new spiritual practices or stick to your current ones?

Would you rather take a mindfulness course or a positive psychology course?

Would you rather practice gratitude journaling or affirmations?

Would you rather take a course on self-love or self-acceptance?

Would you rather practice meditation or journaling for self-reflection?

Would you rather attend a silent retreat or a creativity workshop?

Would you rather take a course on spirituality or a course on personal finance?

Would you rather practice gratitude or generosity as a spiritual practice?

Would you rather join a community group or attend a personal development program?

Would you rather practice mindfulness or self-compassion in your daily life?

Would you rather practice forgiveness or letting go of attachment in relationships?

Would you rather take a course on personal growth or a course on professional development?

Would you rather practice affirmations or visualization techniques for manifesting your goals?

Would you rather attend a spiritual retreat or a couple's therapy program?

Would you rather practice yoga or martial arts for physical and spiritual balance?

Would you rather attend a workshop on self-awareness or a workshop on emotional intelligence?

Dreams & Goals

Would you rather pursue individual career goals or work towards a common career goal?

Would you rather prioritize financial stability or taking risks to pursue your dreams?

Would you rather live in the city or in the countryside to achieve your dreams?

Would you rather have a long-term goal or achieve short-term goals consistently?

Would you rather work towards financial independence or work towards achieving your dreams?

Would you rather work for a non-profit organization or start your own non-profit?

Would you rather take a sabbatical to pursue your dreams or continue working towards them while balancing your job?

Would you rather prioritize your own goals or support your partner's goals first?

Would you rather prioritize family life or pursue individual dreams?

Would you rather have a stable job or take a risk to pursue your passions?

Would you rather achieve one big dream or accomplish several smaller goals?

Would you rather prioritize education or work experience to achieve your career goals?

Would you rather live in a big city or a small town to pursue your dreams?

Would you rather work for a company or be your own boss to achieve your career goals?

Would you rather prioritize financial success or personal fulfillment in achieving your goals?

Would you rather pursue a creative career or a more traditional career?

Would you rather prioritize career advancement or work-life balance in achieving your goals?

Would you rather pursue your dreams or maintain a stable and comfortable lifestyle?

Would you rather focus on short-term goals or long-term vision in achieving your goals?

Would you rather pursue a career that makes a lot of money or a career that makes a positive impact on the world?

Would you rather prioritize material possessions or experiences in pursuing your goals?

Would you rather work towards your goals alone or with a partner?

Would you rather have a mentor or be self-taught in achieving your goals?

Would you rather pursue a career in a field you are passionate about or in a field that offers more financial stability?

Would you rather pursue a high-risk, high-reward path or a low-risk, low-reward path to achieve your goals?

Would you rather achieve your goals quickly or take your time and enjoy the journey?

Would you rather pursue your goals full-time or balance them with other responsibilities?

Would you rather prioritize personal growth or financial success in achieving your goals?

Would you rather pursue a career that aligns with your values or one that offers more prestige and recognition?

Would you rather take a gap year to pursue your dreams or go straight into a career?

Would you rather pursue a traditional career path or blaze your own trail?

Would you rather live in a different country or a different state to pursue your goals?

Would you rather pursue a career that offers flexibility or stability?

Would you rather prioritize short-term gratification or long-term satisfaction in achieving your goals?

Would you rather start a business together or pursue separate careers?

Would you rather work towards a goal that requires sacrifice or compromise?

Would you rather pursue a degree or learn through experience?

Would you rather work towards a goal that benefits your community or benefits you personally?

Would you rather prioritize your physical health or your career goals?

Would you rather prioritize your personal growth or your relationship growth?

Would you rather pursue a goal that challenges you or one that comes naturally to you?

Would you rather invest in your education or your business?

Would you rather pursue a goal that aligns with your values or one that brings you success?

Would you rather focus on goals that benefit your family or goals that benefit your relationship?

Would you rather prioritize your personal passions or your relationship needs?

Would you rather focus on goals that benefit your community or goals that benefit your relationship?

Would you rather pursue a goal that requires collaboration or one that can be achieved independently?

Would you rather focus on goals that benefit your personal growth or your partner's personal growth?

Would you rather pursue a goal that requires financial investment or one that is low-cost?

Would you rather prioritize your spiritual growth or your career goals?

Would you rather pursue a goal that requires leadership or one that allows you to follow?

Would you rather pursue a goal that requires patience or one that can be achieved quickly?

Let's Recap

It is vital to consider how these "would you rather" inquiries can affect a relationship as this book draws to a close. Building trust, increasing closeness, and fostering relationship growth may all be achieved with the simple act of asking thought-provoking questions and conversing openly and honestly.

Through the topics of Trust & Commitment, Conflict, Sex & Intimacy, Work & Money, Family, Fun & Adventure, Growth & Spirituality, and Dreams & Goals, we've explored some of the most crucial aspects of a successful relationship. We've seen how trust is the foundation of any healthy relationship and how it can be strengthened through mutual respect, communication, and commitment. We've learned about conflict resolution and how to navigate disagreements in a constructive and productive way. We've delved into the complexities of sex and intimacy, exploring ways to build a deeper connection and reignite the flames of passion. We've discussed the importance of work and money in a relationship and how to navigate financial disagreements. We've looked at the role of family in a relationship and how to balance individual needs with family obligations. We've explored the importance of fun and adventure, and how to keep the spark alive through shared experiences. We've examined the role of personal growth and spirituality in a relationship and how to support each other's individual journeys. And finally, we've discussed the power of shared dreams and goals in building a strong and lasting bond.

Throughout all these topics, one common thread has emerged: communication is key. By asking each other thought-provoking questions and engaging in open and honest dialogue, couples can deepen their connection, build trust, and create a strong foundation for a successful and fulfilling relationship.

Of course, it's not always easy to engage in this kind of communication. Sometimes, it can be uncomfortable or even scary to bring up sensitive topics. But the more you practice, the easier it becomes. By making a habit of engaging in regular conversations about these topics, you'll find that your relationship grows stronger, and you become more connected to your partner.

Another important takeaway from this book is the importance of balance in a relationship. It's important to balance your individual needs with the needs of the relationship as a whole. This means taking time for yourself, pursuing your own interests, and supporting each other's individual growth and development. At the same time, it's important to make time for each other, to share experiences, and to work together towards shared goals.

Ultimately, the success of a relationship depends on the effort and commitment of both partners. By asking each other these thought-provoking questions, you're taking an important step towards building a strong and lasting bond. But it's important to remember that this is just the beginning. The real work comes in implementing what you've learned, continuing to communicate openly and honestly, and working together towards a shared vision for your future.

So, as you close this book, I encourage you to take what you've learned and put it into practice. Make a habit of engaging in regular conversations about these topics with your partner. Be open, honest, and vulnerable. Listen with an open heart and mind. And most importantly, continue to work together towards a shared vision for your future. With effort, commitment, and a willingness to learn and grow, your relationship can thrive and become stronger with each passing day.

Made in the USA
Las Vegas, NV
30 April 2023

71322667R00056